THE
Spa Bath

Tina Skinner

Schiffer Publishing Ltd

4880 Lower Valley Road, Atglen, Pennsylvania 19310

Courtesy of Manor on Golden Pond, Manchester, New Hampshire

COVER A fire crackles tubside in a romantic stone hearth. *Courtesy of El Dorado Stone*

Schiffer Books are available at special discounts for bulk purchases for sales promotions or premiums. Special editions, including personalized covers, corporate imprints, and excerpts can be created in large quantities for special needs. For more information contact the publisher:

Published by Schiffer Publishing Ltd.
4880 Lower Valley Road
Atglen, PA 19310
Phone: (610) 593-1777; Fax: (610) 593-2002
E-mail: Info@schifferbooks.com

For the largest selection of fine reference books on this and related subjects, please visit our web site at
www.schifferbooks.com
We are always looking for people to write books on new and related subjects. If you have an idea for a book please contact us at the above address.

This book may be purchased from the publisher.
Include $3.95 for shipping.
Please try your bookstore first.
You may write for a free catalog.

In Europe, Schiffer books are distributed by
Bushwood Books
6 Marksbury Ave.
Kew Gardens
Surrey TW9 4JF England
Phone: 44 (0) 20 8392-8585;
Fax: 44 (0) 20 8392-9876
E-mail: info@bushwoodbooks.co.uk
Website: www.bushwoodbooks.co.uk
Free postage in the U.K., Europe; air mail at cost.

Copyright © 2008 by Schiffer Publishing, Ltd.
Library of Congress Control Number: 2007940922

Type set in Novasese Bk Bt/NewBskvll BT

ISBN: 978-0-7643-2953-1
Printed in China

Contents

Courtesy of Coco Palm Resort Dhuni Kolhu, Mali, Maldives

Acknowledgments

Ginger Doyle and Dinah Roseberry for research and editing.

A special thank you to the Angels: Angela Mohr for timeless bath spells and recipes, and Angela Katsigiannis for soaking inspiration.

Introduction

A stream would suffice, or a bucket fresh fetched from the well. With running water, you need only a sink or small shower stall. That's bathing at its most basic. Yet warm water is so much nicer. Soaking in it so soothing. Showering in it so clean. Washing is a simple necessity of civilized life. The financial means to improve the facilities, and the luxury of time, make the bathing ritual one of life's aspirations.

The importance of bathing dates back to ancient cultures. Egyptians bathed to purify themselves before their daily prayers; the Japanese to reconnect with nature; the Romans as a societal ritual. In this book, we'll look at how these traditions live on in the design of our domestic baths, as well as within our psyche.

This isn't meant as an academic study of the bath, however. The wonderful images presented here were gathered to help you plan the bathing area best suited to your needs, aesthetically, practically, and spiritually.

Today's homes often have a master suite complete with a bathroom on a scale our grandparents would never even have dreamed of. Rather than a "water closet," today's contemporary bath is often a full-sized room, or a series of rooms connected to the bedroom. In a contemporary home, one might wander through a long, dress-in closet to an extensive vanity complete with his-and-hers sinks, to a "water closet" with toilet facilities, and to a room complete with a shower stall big enough for four, with multiple water jets capable of spraying in almost every direction. Soaking tubs today come with massaging whirlpool jets, and sometimes with video monitors and sound systems.

The rooms in this book will awe and inspire. Each is packed with ideas for the architectural setting of the room, from columns to cathedral ceilings. Marble, tile, and custom woodwork add value and historic integrity and awe to the settings. This is also an opportunity to study the finer details of the bath setting, from the lighting to the accessories.

The central focus of the bath, the big soaking tub, is explored in a chapter of its own. And a number of sinks and faucets are shown close-up, to help you explore the range of styles available today.

A full whirlpool experience, complete with video, beckons from the corner of this expansive spa bath. *Courtesy of Toll Brothers, Inc.*

Bathing: A History Lesson

Roots in the Roman Bathhouse

Of all the cultures recorded in the annals of human history, ancient Romans were the most flagrant in their infatuation with the bath. Italy is rich in ancient bathhouse architecture, and the Romans built their bathhouses wherever they went. For instance, Bath, England, is renown for the remains of an elegant bathing facility that still stands in testament to the expansive Roman Empire.

The role of public baths has been recorded by archeologists in ancient Egypt and Greece, but the evolution from small, community bath to grand owes credit to the Roman Empire. The introduction of public baths on a grand scale began as early as 81 AD.

Bathhouses were public projects in ancient times, and the government had responsibility for providing recreation for its citizens. Though the Romans engineered incredible aqueducts to supply their cities with water, running water in individual homes was unheard of. Bathhouses were often the pet project of the emperor, and were often the most splendid, and expensive, of the imperial works. Besides ingenious systems for heating the rooms, and for creating steam for steam baths, the Romans lavished lots of extras on their bathhouses – rich furnishings, colored mosaics and paintings, marble panels, and silver faucets and fittings, all set within the amazing architecture pioneered by the Italians, with grand columns and vaulted ceilings.

Admission to the baths was kept very low in order to appease a demanding populace. And they came in droves. There are estimates by historians as to the capacity of some of the bathhouses ranging from 3,000 to 16,000. A Roman bath was generally preceded by exercise, and the ritual would then include several stages of cold and hot baths, scraping, and anointing with oil. However, the Romans came to the bathhouse for far more than physical ritual.

The bathhouse in Rome was much more than a place to bathe, though. With its heat, it sometimes served as a refuge from cold. In summer, there was a place to swim. Year round, it was a place where many citizens passed the bulk of their days. There were feasts, performances, a library, and the chance to gather in a public forum, to companionship and discussion. Life at the bath has been equated to the social scene at the beach – a holiday atmosphere prevailed, with a mix of culture and frivolity.

The Roman bathhouse, and bathing in general, met its demise in Europe during the rise of Christian influence, which condemned bathing as a sin of the flesh. It took more than a millennium for bathing to come back in style. It was actually considered unhealthy during the Middle Ages and the Renaissance.

THE GLORY OF ROME A tub sits center stage within its own classic pavilion, warmed by a fire doubly reflected in an expansive mirror. Marble and tile complete the sense of Roman splendor. *Courtesy of Hermitage Kitchen Design Gallery*

EURO STYLE The French pay tribute to Roman influence in the decorative surround of a round soaking tub. *Courtesy of Chateau de Fere, Fere En Tardenois, France*

WILD WILD WATER Two cowboys revel in their retreat, where dad tries out a copper tub. Family bathing through the turn of the century involved pumping water by hand, heating it on a stove, and filling a tub that everyone would, in turn, share. The hierarchy of age generally dictated the order of bathing, with the youngest enjoying the bathwater last. The water at this point, though, might be so filthy, that the saying developed: "Don't throw out the baby with the bathwater,"—jokingly referring to the murkiness of the tub's contents. *Courtesy of Diamond Spas*

A PIECE OF HISTORY This unique bathroom features a Turkish influence, which spread across the Mediterranean with the expansion of the Ottoman Empire. *Courtesy of Villa Crespi, Orta San Giulio, Italy*

QUIET STUDY An old-fashioned copper tub bubbles with therapeutic air jets. The paneled study sets the stage for a contemporary cowboy to unwind. *Courtesy of Aquatic Industries, Inc.*

Keeping one's hands and face presentable, and undertaking a simple scrubbing once a month was considered sufficient for most civilized Westerners up through the early 1900s. Wash basins and pitchers served the daily sanitary needs, and a copper tub served for a more thorough monthly washing.

The discovery of germs in the mid-1800s helped create a turning point in the attitude toward cleanliness in Western cultures. The private bath, complete with tub, began to find its way into the finer homes around this time.

Asian Sensibilities

Today, as it has for centuries, bathing is an integral part of Japanese culture. Though private baths now enjoy a place in the Japanese home, the public bath (sento) and hot spring resort bath (onsen) are still enjoyed by many. Soaking together is a treasured ritual, and bathing is an essential part of the daily routine.

A Japanese bath centers around a big tub filled with water heated to the point of almost unbearable. This water is not entered until one is clean. Rather, the body is first washed outside the bath, using a bowl to scoop water from the tub to wash oneself before climbing in to soak away one's cares. The fact that a bath is often shared accounts for this preservation of the cleanliness of the main soaking tub. But the bath is about much more than being clean.

After shedding clothes and dirt, one then submerges themselves chin-deep and endeavors to shed care. The environment of piping hot water provides a conduit to relaxation, contemplation, and a sense of well-being and harmony. This harmony includes one's relationship to nature, and whenever possible, the tub overlooks a garden, incorporates a skylight, or in some way brings reminders of Nature into the environment.

Books have been written about the Japanese bath. Throughout this book, the influence of Japanese design and sensibility is mirrored in new products inspired by this ancient ritual.

Courtesy of Aquapal U.S.A.

Asian Mysticism and "The Spa"

Today's busy woman is enticed to escape to a spa in order to restore herself spiritually and physically. The same experience is often evoked at home, with the aid of deep tubs, aromatic oils, and bubbling "bath bombs."

Interestingly, traditions exist throughout Asia of casting magic spells and creating mystical auras in the process of taking a bath. Floral baths, used throughout Southeast Asia, might be used to attract money, the right husband, or pregnancy. The right blend can create good luck in an upcoming game of mahjong.

Though most Western bathers haven't been steeped in such superstitions, we're certainly assaulted with a host of "beauty" industry products that promise stress reduction, romance, and more. Perhaps, through the simple process of reading a label, and then soaking in meditative thoughts and wishes for something, we are able to self-actualize the desired result.

FOR LOVE OF FLOWERS Paradise might be defined as a place where one can pick fresh flowers year round, in such abundance that they can be bathed in! *Courtesy of Hotel De La Paix, Siem Reap, Cambodia*

SET IN STONE A drum-like tub was given a rustic setting, providing an escape from the present day. *Courtesy of Diamond Spas*

GETTING PERSONAL Bubbles, beautiful blooms, and transporting aromas aid you in achieving personal transformation. *Courtesy of the Londra Palace Hotel, Italy*

Prelude to Romance

Without dwelling too long on the sexual appeal of a clean, well-scented body, bathing is certainly a pleasant precursor to a romantic encounter. Romance kits often contain bubble baths. Back scrubs are a lovely method of foreplay. A tub big enough for two enables a couple to escape into another realm together, to shed their otherworldly cares and to come together in a watery world of their own creation.

TANDEM TUB Candlelight and bubbles allow for a hint of mystery in a tub spacious enough for an intimate two. *Courtesy of Ngala Game Reserve, Skukuza, South Africa*

STAIRWAY TO HEAVEN The ascent to a soaking tub gives it a sense of the ethereal. In a place elevated and removed, the space has been hallowed for relaxation. *Courtesy of DiLeonardo International, Inc.*

WAXING ROMANTIC Candlelight has an enchanting effect on the body, casting a warm glow that complements skin tones and creates dancing shadows. *Courtesy of The Log House & Homestead*

Health Benefits of Bathing

Deep Salt Soaks

Doctors recommend bath salts for many ailments, ranging from muscle and bone pain to skin maladies. A soak in salt can alleviate pain from sore muscles and arthritis, and even minor injuries. Salts work to purify the skin, removing dirt, sweat, and toxins as they work in unison with warm water to open pores. Salts can make dry skin softer and suppler, and can improve irritation from eczema, psoriasis, athlete's foot, and insect bites. Salt baths can even help improve your circulation.

It's as easy as sprinkling Epsom salt into warm water, but you can get much more elaborate. Wonderful salt baths are sold over the counter, and seem anything but medicinal with all their wonderful fragrances and attractive applications. A salt bath is also easy and inexpensive to concoct on your own. There are many free recipes on the internet, as well as great books you can buy with recipes for making salts, bath oils, and bath bombs. Here is a basic, therapeutic salt bath recipe you can build on to create the aroma that transports you to the right place. If you have leftovers, it makes a great gift.

Courtesy of Inkaterra, Manchu Picchu, Peru

Heating Up for Health

Today's medical community uses "hydrotherapy" as a term to encompass the use of warm water and jet massage to address conditions including chronic joint and pain and cardiovascular disease. An extended soak in hot water improves circulation and consequently the health of the skin. More importantly, the time spent in a hot tub tackles the problem of stress, thus taking aim at the root cause of many health conditions.

Today's whirlpool tubs and hot tub spas come with a vast array of options. In jets alone, consumers can choose from combinations of whirlpool jets that concentrate pressure, mini jets grouped into clusters, pillow jets that combine massage action with a head rest, shoulder jets,

Courtesy of Blanket Bay, Queenstown, New Zealand

recipe

Basic Salt Soak

2 parts fine Kosher or sea salt

1 part Epsom salt

1 part liquid glycerin (optional)

Essential oil measured in drops (optional)

Food coloring measured in drops (optional)

Mix well until all major clumps are broken up. If you are storing, allow mixture to air dry for an hour or two before storing in a decorative glass container.

Sprinkle half a cup or more in bath water as needed. Don't wash hair in this mixture as it can be drying.

and swirl and moving massage jets that sweep and circle to create a broad area of massage therapy.

The cost of hot tubs is well within the means of most middle-class families today, and many homes incorporate a hot tub room or sunroom for this amenity. Additionally, many homeowners place their hot tub outside, on a deck or in a pavilion, or even under the open sky, for a pleasurable experience even in the midst of a snow shower.

Esteemed Steam

The ancient Romans recognized the purification potential of steam, and treated themselves to steam baths as part of a daily bath ritual. Native Americans did the same as part of a spiritual ritual of purification. The Turks adopted the practice as the Ottoman Empire expanded its influence and engulfed the Mediterranean. The "hammam" public baths became a focal point of many Middle Eastern cultures and, as the Middle East was conquered by Northern Europeans, the "Turkish bath" in a steam room became wildly popular.

Today, steam baths are most commonly found in health clubs and high-end hotels. However, a number of manufacturers are endeavoring to bring the experience into homes.

Medically, steam bathing is recognized for its ability to treat a number of ailments including cardiovascular disease and hypertension, chronic pain, respiratory conditions, and even mild depression and nicotine addiction.

ABOVE: Various jets are programmable to work from every angle, on every body part. *Courtesy of Chateau de Fere, Fere En Tardenois, France*

PERSONAL SAUNA A specially outfitted shower offers a steam bath at the touch of a button, in addition to light and music options, and aromatherapy in which essential oils are distributed via droplets released into the steamhead. *Courtesy of ThermaSol*

A water jet device makes this the perfect place to take a few cardio-vascular laps. In the evening, heat it up to soothe sore muscles and erase the day's tensions. *Courtesy of Diamond Spas*

STAY-AT-HOME SPA A hot tub spa is well within the means of today's middle-class homeowners, and is an easy way to own the "home spa" experience. *Courtesy of Villa Rolundi Gourmet Beach Cancun, Mexico*

Bath Time is Fun Time

As the mother of two young children, I am experiencing the joy of bathing through the eyes of innocents. I can put a cranky child into a warm tub of water and the tension of an entire household dissipates. Within minutes, if not seconds, that cranky child is singing.

Here's a very important lesson: those cranky children generally resist bath time tooth and nail. It takes an escalation of the cranky to get them into the tub. However, it's even tougher to get a "quick" bath in, as it's very hard to get the child back out.

Another mother, describing a difficult phase in her young daughter's life, told me of the family prescription. That daughter was ordered into the tub, and told she couldn't come out until her fingers were little raisins. Invariably, she emerged a little wrinkly, and a lot more pleasant to be around.

Bath time is lots of fun, to paraphrase a Sesame Street character. If you have trouble creating time for your own home spa treatment, it might be worth recalling the most basic of childhood lessons. Get yourself into the tub and don't come out till you're soaked and wrinkled!

> There's no half-singing in the shower. You're either a rock star, or an opera diva.
>
> JOSH GROBAN
> SINGER/SONGWRITER

spa tip

Make Bathtime Fun!

There are dozens of ways to lighten up a bathroom to ensure that you *and* your kids enjoy spending time in the tub.

- Choose a bright or patterned shower curtain, or if your décor is subdued, a fun plastic liner.

- Tissue boxes, shampoo bottles, and bath poufs and loofahs all come in fun and funky shades and interesting packaging.

- When your kids are done bathing, don't hide all of their toys under the sink until next time. Leave a nice toy or two on the tub; it will bring a smile to your face every morning when you hop in for your grown-up shower.

- Cheerful scents like orange, mango, pineapple and coconut create a sunny, tropical, light-hearted mood, in addition to serving as pick-me-ups for early risers.

recipe

No-More-Tears Bubble Bath

1/2 cup no-tears baby shampoo

1 1/2 cups water

1/3 cup corn syrup

Food coloring

Combine shampoo, water and corn syrup and let any bubbles settle. Pour slowly into empty jars or shampoo bottles, then add a few drops of your favorite food coloring. Draw bath as normal, adding a little of the bubble bath directly under the faucet as the tub fills.

RUBBER DUCKY, YOU'RE THE ONE... Can you hum Ernie's song, "Rubber Ducky"? If not, you may be missing out on one of life's most important lessons. *Courtesy of The Inn at Stockbridge*

Components of the Bath

The home spa often doubles as the master bath in today's luxury home. In designing this escape within the home, the dream usually starts with the tub, then proceeds to the other amenities chosen for their aesthetics, efficiency, and practicality. We'll examine them the other way around, saving the best for last.

Showers

Today's showers are much more sophisticated than the old dial-a-jet shower heads of yesteryear. Besides a wonderful array of enclosure options, the technology allows for multiple heads and sophisticated temperature controls, among other features. The following are some samples of options available in home design today.

HIS AND HERS For a busy couple on the go, dual showers with individual controls allow them to dial in their preferences and angle their water jets for the ultimate personal experience. Square jet heads can be focused from the sides and above. *Courtesy of Kohler®*

THROUGH THE LOOKING GLASS A glass enclosure allows the homeowner to slip into a different dimension, with total control over temperature and a host of shower sources. *Courtesy of Kohler®*

Courtesy of Ca Sagredo Hotel, Venice, Italy

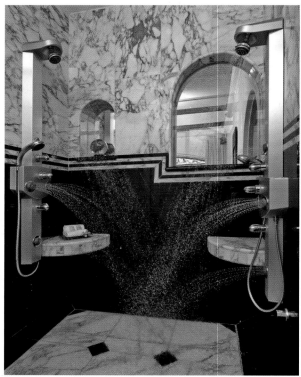

Courtesy of Villa Rolundi Gourmet Beach Cancun, Mexico

BENCH-WARMER A bench seat is easily adjusted to satisfy individual preferences. *Courtesy of Kohler®*

Courtesy of I Casali di Monticchio, Allerno, Italy

Courtesy of Le Hostellerie Marechal, Colmar, France

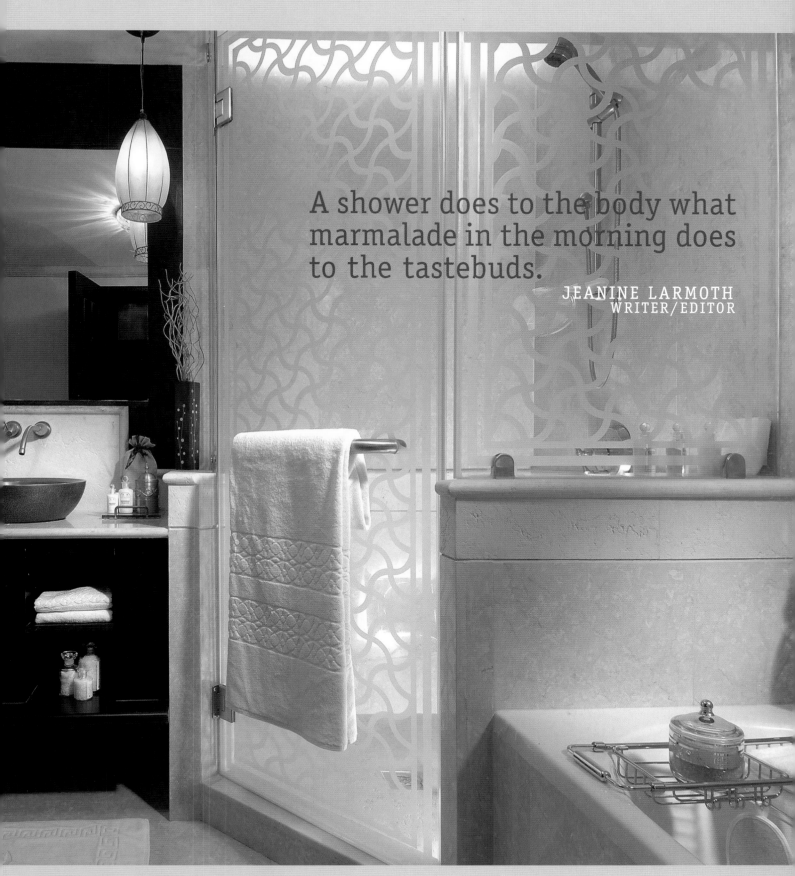

A shower does to the body what marmalade in the morning does to the tastebuds.

JEANINE LARMOTH
WRITER/EDITOR

BEIGE BEAUTY Frosted glass adds sparkle to a room outfitted in soothing neutral tones.
Courtesy of DiLeonardo International, Inc.

Courtesy of Gaia Hotel, Quepos, Costa Rica

Courtesy of Villa Crespi, Orta San Giulio, Italy

BUILDING BLOCKS Glass tile defines a semi-private shower area. Next door, a whirlpool tub nests in a surround of clean tile, warmed by sunshine via windows that encompass both water and sky views. *Courtesy of Porcher© American Standard*

Today's master suite is furnished with custom pieces destined to become heirlooms.
Courtesy of DuraSupreme Cabinetry

Sinks

Designers and manufacturers are in a flat-out race to outdo each other in refashioning the sink. Today, the sink might take any form, be it above or below the countertop surface. These imaginative basins are served by hardware equally as inventive. This section is not intended as a serious survey of today's innovative offerings. Rather, it serves as a small sampling while focusing more on the larger picture of vanities fashioned for the master bath.

Courtesy of Kohler®

Courtesy of Kohler®

Courtesy of Hotelito Desconodico, Puerto Vallarta, Mexico

Courtesy of Sivoy Punta Cana Beach, Punta Cana, Dominican Republic

Courtesy of Eichardts Private Hotel, Queenstown, New Zealand

Photography by Dan Muro, Fast Forward Unlimited

Courtesy of Aquapura Douro Valley, Lemego, Portugal

Photography by Dave Adams Photography, Courtesy of Joyce Hoshall Interiors

Photography by Dan Muro, Fast Forward Unlimited, Courtesy of Plumberry Designs, Inc.

MIRROR, MIRROR Lighting mirrors a custom vanity in this elegant suite. *Courtesy of DiLeonardo International, Inc.*

Art Deco sensibilities are evoked in his-and-hers vanity, with sparkly glass bowls forming a focal point. *Courtesy of Hermitage Kitchen Design Gallery*

Courtesy of Lacava, LLC

Courtesy of Ngala Game Reserve, Skukuza, South Africa

KEEP ME COMPANY This lovely suite illustrates the trend toward transforming the bath into a room where one, or two, can linger. When the Kohler Company came to the forefront in the 1920s, it was encouraging consumers to transform a closet in their home into a bathroom, thus moving away from the "outhouse." Today, sink fixtures are part of fine furnishings, and the master bathroom is becoming a space that can actually boast square footage in a real estate write-up. *Courtesy of Kohler®*

Courtesy of Kohler®

ON SAFARI Exotica reigns in the bathroom above, with animal prints, hand-crafted glass, and a golden glow. *Courtesy of All American Design & Furnishings, Inc.*

Courtesy of Die Hirschgrasse, Heidelberg, Germany

Courtesy of Evanson 6 Senses, Oman, Middle East

Courtesy of Inkaterra, Manchu Picchu, Peru

Courtesy of Le Hotel Regina, Warsaw, Poland

Courtesy of Lacava, LLC

The Spa Bath | 27

Courtesy of Aquapura Douro Valley, Lemego, Portugal

Courtesy of Moen, Inc.

Courtesy of La Sultana 'Marrakech' Hotel & Spa, Marrakech, Africa

Courtesy of Aka Hotel Resort & Spa, Hua Hin, Thailand

SEEING DOUBLE As opposed to putting one sink and vanity in today's new master bath suites, designers tend to install two. His-and-hers sink options open the possibility of two getting their toilettes done simultaneously, and lessen the possibility of resentment against the "bathroom hog" who takes too much time at the sink. The extended vanity also provides a lot more storage and display space, and in an extensive *"bath room"* the cabinetry is an important feature. *Courtesy of Diamond Spas*

The Tub

The tub is the big space hog in the master-bath suite. In terms of space and budget, the tub gets most of the initial consideration. The following section explores various kinds of tub designs, and showcases unique tubs for those hoping to immerse themselves in something unusual.

Tub Surrounds

The standard treatment of the custom tub installation is a surround. Practically, the surround is a wonderful way to disguise plumbing. Many tubs are designed to be hidden with the exception of the ledge and interior. A surround, however, can go beyond its simple functional need. It can be expanded to create a ledge for seating and a place to set the toiletries – bubble bath, salts, sponges, scrubbies, and soft towels – within easy reach. For the homeowner, though, its importance lies in its ability to embrace the tub, like a jewel within a setting, and to establish the importance of the tub, throne-like, within the bath.

WARM WATER A good soak, fireside, is medicine for the soul. *Courtesy of Eldorado Stone*

Courtesy of Aquatic Industries, Inc.

Courtesy of Aquatic Industries, Inc.

NOW YOU SEE ME Textured glass fills a window between soaking tub and built-in shower, allowing some natural light to filter into the stall. The tub's nook, overlooked by shuttered windows, offers a wonderful sense of seclusion. *Courtesy of Hermitage Kitchen Design Gallery*

Courtesy of Divine Kitchens

Courtesy of Jacuzzi Whirlpool Bath

SPOTLESS SPA A clean, uncluttered place reflects the mindset of the soul bathing here. *Courtesy of a karen black company*

Freestanding Tubs

Freestanding tubs are designed to stand alone within a room. Their shapely forms are carefully designed both inside and out. Traditionally, these tubs might have a ringed bottom, or a flare. Their cousins, the footed tubs, follow in the next section.

Courtesy of Nafplia Palace, Greece

Courtesy of Langshott Manor, London, England

Courtesy of The Oberoi Amarvilas, Uttar Pradesh, India

Courtesy of Aquatic Industries, Inc.

Footed Tubs

The claw-foot tub was first manufactured by American Standard in the late 1800s. Cast in iron, it was coated in enamel to make it easier to clean. It soon fell out of favor, but antique footed tubs are very much in demand, and new ones are being manufactured and offered on the specialty market. Perfect for a historic property, footed tubs hold a place in the imagination that harkens back to a romantic past. A footed tub seems to elevate the soaker above life's common cares.

Courtesy of Loch Torridon Country House Hotel, Achnasheen, England

Courtesy of The Bath Priory Hotel, Berkshire, England

Courtesy of Langshott Manor, London, England

Courtesy of Loch Torridon Country House Hotel, Achnasheen, England

Courtesy of Albergo Piet, Pietransanta, Italy

Courtesy of Hotel San Georgio, PortoFino, Italy

Sunken Tubs

A sunken tub presents some design challenges as it requires a raised floor or a lot of clearance below. The whole idea of "sinking" into the tub, though, has huge appeal.

Photography by Dave Adams Photography; Courtesy of Joyce Hoshall Interiors

Courtesy of The Oberoi Mauritius, Mauritius, Indian Ocean

Courtesy of Sila Evanson Hideaway & Spa at Samui, Koh Samui Suratthani, Thailand

ISLAND PARADISE A square, stainless tub reigns over a delightful, tropical garden setting. *Courtesy of Diamond Spas*

Unique Tubs

Take a delightful look at unique tubs that are not likely to be found in your local design showroom. There's a world of ideas out there, waiting to make your bathing experience unique and perfectly suited to your home spa.

FALL IN LOVE ALL OVER AGAIN A glass tub fed by a waterfall is a great opportunity for a mind-clearing soak. *Courtesy of The Forbury Hotel, Berkshire, England*

A PENNY SAVED A copper bath was created specifically to fit the interior of a remodeled grain silo for a unique bathing experience. *Photography by Peter Wnek, Courtesy of Diamond Spas*

STEEL AWAY Candles illuminate a deep, stainless steel Japanese bath with a bowed top ledge.
Photography by Tom Henry; Architect/Designer Tim Bjella, Courtesy of Diamond Spas / Trends Publishing International

Courtesy of Lacava, LLC

Courtesy of The Bale Resort & Spa, Denpasur Bali, Indonesia

Courtesy of The Sandpiper, Bridgetown, Barbados, Caribbean

HIGH-DEF SOAK Minimalism is maximized in a bath suite furnished with a solid marble tub and a flat-screen TV. *Courtesy of LimeStone Gallery*

CONCRETE TRUTH A concrete soaking tub brings an organic element to the bath. *Courtesy of Eldorado Stone*

The Spa Bath | **43**

Tub Settings

No less important than the choice of a tub, is how it is situated within the bath. The tub's surroundings form your scenery. The more pleasant the scenery, the longer you'll want to linger.

CANOPY CLEAN A four-poster tub with canopy adds unique appeal to this bathing experience. *Courtesy of Langshott Manor, London, England*

LIMESTONE LUXURY A tub fashioned from solid basalt. *Courtesy of LimeStone Gallery*

A MOMENT WITH THE MOUNTAINS A comfy tub nestles next to a powerful view in a master suite rich in architectural elegance. *Courtesy of Toll Brothers, Inc.*

Window Seats

A bath with a view is a most desirable configuration in today's master-bath suite. We've all enjoyed a view from our kitchen window, usually with peeks snatched while doing an odious chore such as washing dishes. Why not a view where one is stationary in the most relaxing place and position possible? Natural light adds to the appeal by day, and good shutters or curtains ensure privacy by night.

THREE'S COMPANY Wall-length mirrors on either side triple the effect of a large, decorative window in this wonderful bath space. *Courtesy of Toll Brothers, Inc.*

Courtesy of Toll Brothers, Inc.

There must be quite a lot of sorrows
that cannot be cured by a hot bath,
but I don't know any of them.

SYLVIA PLATH
AMERICAN POET

Courtesy of Labiz Silhouette, Make, Kenya, Africa

Courtesy of Nafplia Palace, Greece

GREEN WITH ENVY Green tile unifies an elegant white retreat, where an oval soaking tub offers to caress away all cares. *Photography by Dave Adams Photography, Courtesy of Reynolds Gualco Architecture-Interior Design*

Courtesy of Grasmere Lodge, Christchurch, New Zealand

Every man has the right to a Saturday night bath.

LYNDON B. JOHNSON
AMERICAN PRESIDENT

CREATING WITH COPPER Off a master bedroom suite a copper tub commands a small bump-out with an incredible view. *Courtesy of Diamond Spas*

Courtesy of Porcher© American Standard

Courtesy of Residenza Del Moro, Firenze, Italy

Courtesy of Toll Brothers, Inc.

Bathing Al Fresco

Back to basics, a good soak outside is a chance to get in touch with nature. Whether illuminated by stars or sun, clement weather and warm water are an alluring invitation.

Courtesy of Qualia, Hayman Island, Australia

Courtesy of Island Hideaway Resort & Spa, Dhonakulhi, Maldives

RIGHT *Courtesy of Post Ranch, Monterey, California*

BELOW *Courtesy of Katitche Point Guesthouse, The Valley, British Virgin Islands*

ROMANCE & RENEWAL Bathing *al fresco* in a hot bath complete with massaging jets is the ultimate in romantic ideals. *Courtesy of MTI Whirlpools*

Fireside

Fire and water are two elements that soothe and relax mankind. Short of a seaside getaway, a big tub full of water helps satisfy the need to be next to a big body of water. A fireplace doubles the delightful effect.

Today's fireplace manufacturers have made installation a breeze, often without a chimney. Gas and electric fireplaces eliminate the need to haul and store messy firewood, too, so a fireplace becomes much more practical in a room like the bathroom.

THINKING OUTSIDE THE FIRE Stacked wood provides everything but the crackle in evoking the image of fire and fireplace. The central tub basks in the imaginary glow amidst a paneled bath perfect for contemporary Colonial sensibilities. *Courtesy of Kohler®*

ALL-NATURAL Stone was carefully installed to form a ledge overlapping a copper soaking tub. A waterfall and a fireplace add delight to the entire experience. *Photography by Tom Beckering Photography, Designer: High Camp Home/High Sierra Customs, Courtesy of Diamond Spas*

Corner Tubs

Besides claiming a position of power for the tub, corner placement can help maximize space in a smaller bath. One way to wedge more spa-like amenities into a small or midsize bath suite is to utilize the corners. The goal, in most cases, is more bathing space for a deeper, more satisfying bath.

Courtesy of Gastineau Log Homes, Inc.

HEAVENLY HUES White, white, and more white gives this cathedral-like space its *cleanliness is next to Godliness* appeal. Soft towels and a warm bath are the ultimate angelic escape. *Photography by Bob Splichal RS Photography, Courtesy of The Log House & Homestead*

A FISHERMAN'S FIXTURES Trout swim upstream on a custom vanity, while a small pond awaits, filling with warm water and bubbles. *Courtesy of Gastineau Log Homes, Inc.*

Courtesy of Ashdown Park, East Sussex, England

Courtesy of Belle Epoque, Baden Baden, Germany

Tub Alcoves

Another way to maximize the size of the tub is to build a bump-out addition on the home, or to design a nook with a big whirlpool tub in mind. Here is a chance to see some nooks close-up. Many more are to be found in the gallery that follows.

Courtesy of Harbour Village, Beach Club Netherlands Antilles, Bonaire

Courtesy of Inn of 5 Graces, Santa Fe, NM

Photography by Roger Wade, Courtesy of Barna Log Homes

Incredible Spa Baths: A Guided Tour

If a picture speaks a thousand words, the following pages are an encyclopedia of ideas. Journey through private retreats that embody the best in today's bathroom projects, presented by manufacturers and designers around the world. We'll start with modestly-sized suites and advance to those of palatial proportions. Enjoy. You are sure to find ideas that are perfect for the space you have, or plan to build.

CHANGE COLOR Copper and stone team up for a unique bathing experience. *Courtesy of Diamond Spas*

ABOVE Lights and mirrors lend their magic to a small room outfitted nicely for a big soak. *Courtesy of DiLeonardo International, Inc.*

RIGHT A granite countertop on the expansive vanity matches that surrounding the inviting whirlpool tub. *Courtesy of Hermitage Kitchen Design Gallery*

Courtesy of Le Hostellerie Marachal, Colmar, France

Courtesy of The Raj Palace, Jaipur, India

Courtesy of Petit Palais Hotel de Charm, Milan, Italy

Courtesy of Riverside, Prague, Poland

spa tip

Designing with Safety in Mind

The bathroom can be a pretty dangerous place, according to the United State's National Safety Council, which reports that nearly 200,000 people are injured annually in America within their bathrooms. To help minimize risk, consider some of the recommendations made by the National Kitchen & Bath Association, including:

○ Use slip-resistant flooring throughout the bathroom, as well as in the tub and shower.

○ A platform surrounding the tub will allow you to sit upon entering and exiting.

○ Use shatterproof glass in shower doors.

○ Maintain safe distances between water sources and electrical switches.

○ Use cabinet locks on storage where poisonous household products or prescription medicines are stored.

Courtesy of Savoy Moscow Hotel, Moscow, Russia

GOING GREEN Concrete forms a contemporary surround, finished to stone-like perfection and stained to a fanciful shade chosen for a discerning client. *Courtesy of SF Janes Architects, Inc.*

Courtesy of Cortijo Soto Real, Seville, Spain

Courtesy of Ashdown Park, East Sussex, England

GIRL'S NIGHT IN A romantic, feminine retreat in pink and green provides a haven for the lady of the house. The tub becomes an architectural element, paneled below and framed by columns supporting a dropped ceiling within a cathedral roofline. *Courtesy of Maureen Fiori and Bonnie Hafnagel, CKD*

Custom cabinetry makes it possible to match tub surround to a corner vanity unit. *Courtesy of Wellborn Forest*

Courtesy of Old Bahama Bay, West End, Bahamas

spa tip

Choosing a Designer

The National Kitchen & Bath Association, which trains and accredits professional designers, offers some suggestions to consumers planning a remodel. Remodeling the bath is "not a do-it-yourself project," the NKBA advises. Specialized professionals should be consulted to make accurate measurements and to design a functional, safe, and cost-efficient space. They suggest that you:

○ Interview several designers in your area, and trade ideas and suggestions.

○ Ask to see the professional's portfolio, visit their showroom, and ask for a list of references.

○ Determine that they have a friendly, helpful staff in order to ensure an enjoyable experience.

○ The NKBA certifies designers as follows:
  AKBD Associate Kitchen & Bath Designer;
  CKD Certified Kitchen Designer;
  CBD Certified Bathroom Designer, and
  CMKBD Certified Master Kitchen & Bath Designer

To find a member near you or to receive your free NKBA Kitchen and Bath Consumer Workbook, call (800) THE-NKBA or visit www.nkba.org.

MACHO MAN A man can awake feeling like master of the universe in this masculine, marble-lined bath, made sleeker with chrome, stainless steel, and artisan glass. *Photography: Dan Muro, Fast Forward Unlimited, Courtesy of Plumberry Designs, Inc.*

HIP TO BE SQUARE An ultra-contemporary bathroom provides a new view on the room's potential. A square tub in stainless steel affords the latest technology for a deep soaking, and Japanese sensibilities are evoked in a stepped storage unit. The toilet doubles as a bench when not in use. *Courtesy of Julien, Troy Adams Design™*

A floor-to-ceiling picture window provides the connection to nature essential to the Japanese aesthetic. *Courtesy of Aquatic Industries, Inc.*

Natural stone and stainless steel team up for a contemporary bath offering the latest in luxury. *Courtesy of Atlanta Design & Build*

High-Tech Extras

As we continue to create snazzier, more high-tech gadgetry to listen to music, watch movies, and make phone calls, our bathroom is in no way being left behind. Your budget will determine the extent of your final home spa experience, but these cool custom spa gadgets will help upgrade your space and your experience.

NICE AND TOASTY A heated floor is a wonderful amenity in a bath, and certainly not an afterthought. It will be one of the first things installed in new construction or a remodel. Heat lamps, likewise, can add to the comfort level of the room, and warm towels are a decadent luxury you'll want to wrap yourself up in.

IN A FOG? While you're heating things up, you might want to think about clearing the air. Fog-free mirrors cut out the frustration of not seeing yourself after a steamy bath or shower.

GET CONNECTED If you'll be lingering long, you might want to include music, video, or cable entertainments. And you might want to link the room up via intercom or telephone with the outside world.

A marbled counter sits beneath twin vanity mirrors and reflected sink fixtures that repeat the stainless steel concept and complete the look. *Courtesy of Atlanta Design & Build*

NATURAL RESOURCES Granite countertop, marble tile, and custom woodwork unify an expansive bath, with soaking tub and multi-jet shower. A leaded glass window filters sunlight while providing privacy and a focal point. *Courtesy of Atlanta Design & Build*

RISING EMPIRE Multiple tones of marble and antique finish evoke a classic Roman bath, fit for an emperor. *Photography by Dave Adams Photography, Courtesy of Joyce Hoshall Interiors*

recipe

Turn Stress into Rubble

2-3 Tablespoons of a favorite bubble bath

1 cup sea salt

Mix thorughly, then sift under running bathwater. Light several white and pink candles, the colors of self-love and kindness, and whisper this comforting poem:

Bubble, Bubble,
It ain't no trouble.
Caring for myself
turns stress into rubble.

spa tip

A Bit about Universal Design

Buzz in the home design industry abounds regarding "universal design" of homes, particularly the more utilitarian areas like kitchens and baths. Universal design refers to accessibility and ease of use for people of all physical abilities. The idea encompasses physical challenges caused by infirmity or aging.

The Baby Boomer generation is driving today's healthy luxury home market, and though it is not a sexy topic for discussion, there is a recognized need to plan for the onset of age-related issues. In the area of bathroom design, this means a special sensitivity to safety, access, and comfort in the bath. Shower and tub products are proliferating an ease of access for individuals restricted by walkers or wheelchairs.

STRAIGHT OFF THE VINE A lush and playful tomato tone adds warm contrast in a travertine stone tile and glass bath. *Courtesy of Atlanta Design & Build*

Courtesy of Costwold House Hotel, Chipping Campden, England

If I want to be alone — some place I can write,
I can read, I can pray, I can cry, I can do what-
ever I want — I go into the bathroom.

ALICIA KEYS
SINGER/SONGWRITER

BEHIND CLOSED DOORS A galley-shaped bath embodies the best of efficiency. Floor-to-ceiling locker-like storage keeps the ephemera of ablutions out of sight, focusing all attention on the extended view beyond picture windows. *Courtesy of Benning Design Associates, Inc.*

DIFFERENT STRIPES An aura of exotic is added with a zebra skin, while contemporary finishes on woodwork, and a stainless surround for the whirlpool tub ground this wonderful room firmly in the present. *Courtesy of Benning Design Associates, Inc.*

Whether by firelight or twilight, this tub offers delight. *Courtesy of Atlanta Design & Build*

spa tip

A Word About Custom Cabinetry

Consumers are fully aware of cabinet manufacturers' services when it comes to kitchen design and remodeling, but the industry is working hard to get out the word that they do bathrooms, as well. Custom or stock cabinetry often plays a role in a simple vanity. However, cabinetry can be manufactured to match and is a wonderful way to unify a large bathroom suite's design. Storage units, as well as bath surrounds, and even matching wardrobe units can be made to furnish the bath as well as adjacent dressing and sleeping areas.

BUBBLE BATH Circular tile mosaic evokes past and present in a room where a custom, stainless steel tub takes center stage. *Photography by Christopher Ray Photography; Builder: TempleHome, Courtesy of Diamond Spas*

CASCADE A waterfall courses beside a stainless steel soaking tub. Below, glass ensures the sanitary condition of river stones evoking nature in this carefully-crafted retreat. *Photography by William Wright Photography, Courtesy of Diamond Spas*

SAILOR'S DELIGHT A nautical theme unites a crisp, clean, and inviting master-bath suite. All the elements of pleasurable ablution are at hand – clean towels, warm water, and a sense of quiet solitude. *Courtesy of Divine Kitchens*

FIT FOR A QUEEN An expansive alcove off the boudoir offers the lady of the house her own sacred sanctuary.
Photography by Dave Henry Photography, Courtesy of Reynolds Gualco Architecture-Interior Design

recipe

The Bath of Lavender

If you find your day to be filled with tension and mishap, relaxing with a lavender bath may be the way to calm your mind and body. This relaxing remedy should help release tight and stressed musles, as well as fill your senses with floral repose. You will need:

  2 tsp. fresh Lavender

  2 tsp. fresh Chamomile

  2 tsp. fresh Rosemary

  1/2 cup lemon juice (optional)

  Small cloth bag, and ribbon

Place herbs in cloth bag and cinch with ribbon; allow water from the faucet to flow through the sachet into a warm bath. NOTE: Some have sensitivities to various herbal products; this should be explored before taking a lavender bath.

spa tip

Color Me Happy

The color palette you pick for your home spa will set the tone, literally, for your experience there. These tips should get you started:

The majority of people seeking a spa experience want it to be a restful one, so soft tones and subtle neutrals predominate in bath designs.

Cool tones, such as light greens, lavenders, and watery blues, may feel refreshing in an environment steamed up by a whirlpool tub. They are also more inviting in a hot climate.

As a feminine domain, the spa bath is often accented in peaches, pinks, and citrus tones. Deep red brings romance into play, easily achieved with candles and accent textiles and soaps.

White is a favorite bathroom color, with the cleanliness that evokes, and the safety of property "resale" in mind. However, it's important not to use too much, or the room becomes cold. Add warm beiges and golds, and accent with your favorite earthy deep tones: blues, reds, browns, or greens.

There are no bad colors for the bathroom. What's important is that you are surrounded by colors that make you feel good. The goal is a room that is relaxing and uplifting for you.

Courtesy of Manor on Golden Pond, Manchester, NH

Courtesy of Goodstone Estate, Middleburg, VA

Courtesy of Golden Eagle Log Home.

CITY OF LOVE Ivory paneling with an antiqued finish creates a sense of Parisian sophistication in this luxurious bath, outfitted both for relaxation and organization. *Courtesy of Hermitage Kitchen Design Gallery*

recipe

After-Bath Pillow Packet

2 tsp. fresh Lavender leaves

2 tsp. whole cloves

Handkerchief envelope

Place herbs in the envelope and tuck the package into your pillowcase for a soothing way to drift off to sleep after an evening bath, for a rest filled with kind thoughts and pleasant dreams.

Breathing in,
Breathing out,
Heaviness begins to drift.
Breathing in,
Breathing out,
Weariness begins to lift.

LATHER AT THE LODGE Log siding and exposed beams create a rich, rustic environment for getting back to one's roots.
Courtesy of Hearthstone, Inc.

GUEST BATH This room is designed to host a couple, or entertain a best friend. An ottoman wheels to wherever it's needed – tubside for a back washing, or next to the vanity for a chat during the daily ritual. *Photography by Dave Adams Photography, Courtesy of Joyce Hoshall Interiors*

BLONDE BOMBSHELL Mirrors and glass amplify a luxurious master bath, in blonde marble slabs and accented with golden tones. *Photography by Dave Adams Photography, Courtesy of Joyce Hoshall Interiors*

Keep it Handy

Bathrooms evolved from closets, and then the linen closets evolved to a different area of the home. Today, there's no reason to traipse down the hall for a fresh towel. Master-bath suites afford plenty of space for storage, and you can maximize this with cabinetry and shelving.

If you've got the space, a fun idea is a bath cart. Like the cocktail cart of old, a wheeled cart can be pushed next to the tub when you need it, to have scrub sponges, lotions, soaps, and any other bath favorites close at hand. When you're finished, it's easily wheeled out of sight.

SETTLE IN The Colonial aesthetic of old New England is adapted to the newly discovered, ancient soaking rituals of Japan in a bath designed as an escape from the everyday. A copper soaking tub is tucked in a private niche and flanked by sun-filled windows and antiqued cabinetry. Antique-style lantern lighting emulates the landscape of Beacon Hill of the home's exterior. *Courtesy of Lee Kimball*

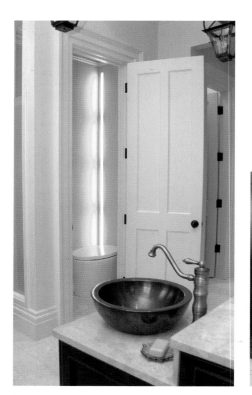

JUST SO Each element of the daily ritual has its place, clearly defined in a bathroom meticulously free of clutter. *Courtesy of Kohler®*

LEMON ZEST A pedestal sink and a tub command their own architectural nooks in a suite outfitted for a long, luxurious ablution. Tiles in two warm, earthy tones provide a backdrop. *Courtesy of Kohler®*

Feminine appeal is married to contemporary simplicity in a bath suite that has it all, including a generously-sized soaking tub for when time permits. *Courtesy of Kohler®*

Courtesy of Dream of Africa, Malindi, Kenya, Africa

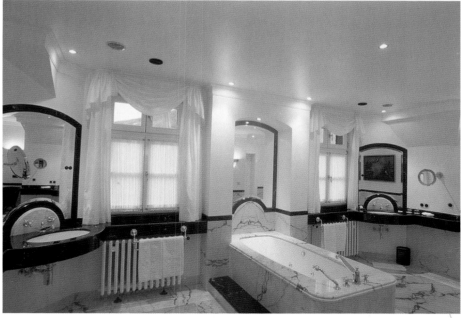

Courtesy of Krone Assmannshausen, Rudensheim, Germany

Courtesy of Villa Rolundi Gourmet Beach Cancun, Mexico

Courtesy of Solitaire Lodge, Rotorua, New Zealand

spa tip

Lean Back!

If you're like most spa bathers, relaxing may mean leaning back. Bath pillows were made for just such a circumstance. Many variations are available to suit your relaxing needs, ranging from inflatable to massaging to aromatherapy inserts. Meant for submersion, they are the perfect cushion between a weary back and a porcelain tub. Be sure to keep your pillow clean and dry when not in use.

When you put your head back, an eye compress or mask comes in handy to shield and soothe weary eyes. Some can be used with hot or cold water, and others even smell of soothing herbs like lavender or mint.

So go ahead, lean back; you deserve it!

Courtesy of Oberoi Vanyavilas, Sawai Madhopur, Rajasthan Prov., India

Courtesy of Hacienda Santos Alamos, Sonora, Mexico

Courtesy of Aquapura Douro Valley, Lemego, Portugal

Courtesy of Huka Lodge, Taupo, New Zealand

Marble creates stages within a surround of wood flooring. *Courtesy of LimeStone Gallery*

Straight lines and warm tones lend a masculine feel to this spacious bath. *Courtesy of Moen, Inc.*

Courtesy of Aquapura Douro Valley, Lemego, Portugal

Keeping it Clean

Trapped water is the enemy of your bath area. It gets under caulking and allows the disintegration of surfaces. Shower organizers that hang toiletries up to dry are a great invention. Be sure to put away washcloths, towels, soaps and bottles, and bathmats after each use to avoid trapped water.

HAVING THE BLUES A half-wall preserves a powerful view, and encases plumbing fixtures. *Courtesy of Moen, Inc.*

recipe

Turn These Events

Oatmeal is awesome, combining fiber and natural fat in one package. Mix this healthy facial pack for a stay-at-home spa experience.

Rolled oats (avoid instant oatmeal, which has been stripped of some of its natural properties)
Avacadoes, or honey (optional)
Mint tea, cooled
Mortar and pestle, or blender / food processor

Pound the rolled oats with the mortar and pestle; you may chop the oats in a blender, but the mortar and pestle method puts more of your personal energy into the process, making it even healthier. Mix the oatmeal with avacadoes or honey, or you may use plain spring water; let your body tell you which ingredients to mix with the oats. Use as a facial wash or masque, and rinse gently with cooled mint tea.

Turn these events, spiral and turn.
Work these events, for the good that I yearn.
That the best shall be for the he and the she,
Turn these events for the good that shall be.

SECRET GARDEN A park bench provides a garden feel for a country-style bath suite furnished with an old-fashioned, footed tub and pair of pedestal sink stands. *Courtesy of Moen, Inc.*

MARBLE MASSAGE A wonderful whirlpool tub with a waterfall and jet massage for the back sits center stage in a bath suite rich in two-toned marble. His-and-hers sinks, an automated toilet/bidet, and state-of-the-art shower top off the upscale features. *Photography by Dan Muro, Fast Forward Unlimited, Courtesy of Plumberry Designs, Inc.*

HOT CHOCOLATE Sophisticated and stylish, rich wood tones warm this contemporary setting, defined by molded wainscoting and featuring a whirlpool tub as the centerpiece. *Courtesy of Porcher© American Standard*

Shared Experience

In Western society, the idea of bathing together is generally reserved for lovers. A humorous slogan during the first round of environmental concern in the 1970s encouraged people to "conserve water, shower with a friend." In Japan, bathing with a friend is considered a bonding act; the Japanese expression *Hadaka no tsukiai* or "naked friendship" is used to express a very deep friendship. Bathing together bonds a friendship, and is free of sexual inference.

GRAY AREA Cool tones add to the crisp feeling of a luxury bath. Because the cabinetry, tile, and fixtures are neutral in tone, it's easy to accessorize and change the look according to whim or season. In this case, a touch of purple adds fantasy. *Photography by Dave Adams Photography, Courtesy of Reynolds Gualco Architecture-Interior Design*

BUILDING BLOCKS Glass block provides light and preserves privacy in an expansive master-bath suite. The room's central features – a whirlpool bath and a chic bowl basin sink – rise above stone surrounds. *Courtesy of Shasta Smith*

BACK IN TIME Repeating arches and architectural columns add to the old-world appeal of this master suite. *Courtesy of Toll Brothers, Inc*

PICTURE PERFECT A shower stall is connected to the tub via a large picture window, allowing both spaces to feel more open. *Courtesy of Toll Brothers, Inc.*

ROUND FOR A REASON The curve of an elegant marble and tile tub surround is mirrored in a glass-block privacy screen. The master suite flows from bath to lavatory to a closet-sized dressing area, an enviable expanse of personal hygiene space. *Courtesy of Toll Brothers, Inc.*

The Spa Bath | 105

Focus on the View

Predetermining what you will look at, and why, can enhance the mind-clearing practice of the bath and amplify the benefits.

If you don't have a window next to your bath, you might want to bring along a view. Books and magazines, ones that you don't mind getting wet, are certainly something you might consider. You might also bring along an image of a friend or family member who needs your good thoughts and prayers, or a vase of flowers to gaze upon. A flickering candle can also focus a mind in need of clearing.

LADY IN RED Red in a woman's sweater, red candlesticks, and a touch of accent in the decorative towels create easily-changed decorative focal points in a spacious master bath with deep soaking tub. *Courtesy of Toll Brothers, Inc.*

OF THE ORIENT A hand-made ceramic tub, crafted in Japan, invites one to immerse themselves in the traditional soaking ritual enjoyed for centuries in Japan. *Courtesy of Aquapal U.S.A.*

spa tip

Detox in a Salt Soak

Many recipes for salt baths blend sea salt, Epsom salt, and baking soda. These ingredients work together to detoxify the skin, drawing out heavy metals, radiation, and foreign objects, while soothing the skin. In return, the skin is even believed to absorb the natural vitamins and minerals found in the sea salt.

For a basic salt soak recipe to get you started, see page 10.

CAVE DWELLING A stream of water and an abstract room allow one, or two, the luxury of escaping into fantasy in a room that can only be described as a contemporary cave. Water fills an oversized copper soaking tub from a ceiling spout, a whimsical touch in a room infused with imagination. *Courtesy of Diamond Spas*

WAVE ON WAVE Fanciful curves play in the warm atmosphere of a tiled and paneled bath suite. *Courtesy of DuraSupreme Cabinetry*

PRINCESS PRIVACY A whimsical tile swirl demarcates a woman's vanity, complete with a pink petal sink. *Courtesy of Kohler®*

FRENCH COUNTRY Lace curtains frame a feminine retreat, while sheers filter the sunlight from a broad bank of windows. Rich upholstery, antique-patterned rugs, and a generous sprinkling of tassels and fringe contribute to the French atmosphere of this bath. *Courtesy of Joyce Hoshall Interiors*

recipe

Make Me Wise

Lemon peel

Fresh mint leaves

Rub your palms together while holding the lemon rind and mint, rubbing their essential oils into your hands. Listening to calming music, hold your hands over your closed eyes, close enough to feel the heat of your palms, but not touching. Enjoy absorbing the aromas and soft warmth while saying:

Enliven my spirit
Open my eyes
Fill me with knowledge
Making me wise.

spa tip

Drinking and Dunking

A glass of wine or an herbal tea are a nice touch to a relaxing bath. Words of caution are in order, though: glass or porcelain should be handled with care in the slippery environment of a bath. Should a glass or cup break into the tub, get out right away and carefully drain and clean the tub with clear water. It's handy to have a pair of slippers nearby in case of broken glass – being naked and barefoot in the vicinity of glass shards is unpleasant!

It goes without saying that too much alcohol and a bath are a very bad combination. You are far more likely to break glasses and bottles, and there's always the risk of falling and hurting yourself, or simply falling asleep in a dangerously deep tub. Enjoy sipping, but stay safe.

STORAGE SURPLUS An antique finish on extensive custom cabinetry in this master-bath suite adds an aura of history and romance to this room. OPPOSITE: An antique hutch reproduction fits in beautifully alongside a modern-day whirlpool bath set in a marble surround. *Photography by Joe Zugcic, Courtesy of Interior Designs by Ria, LLC*

BEAMING FROM EAR TO EAR Wood, stone, and tile define the environment in this expansive master-suite bath. A copper tub and two porcelain urn sink stands provide memorable furnishings. *Courtesy of Hearthstone, Inc.*

Courtesy of Labiz Silhouette, Make, Kenya, Africa

spa tip

Know Your Routine

It's easy to dwell on the fantasy of relaxing hours spent soaking in warm, soapy bubbles. The reality, though, is that you're going to be rushing through most of your visits to the master-bath suite, getting ready for work and social activities.

Separate his-and-hers master baths are becoming standard in high-end homes, but in lieu of this, you'll want to make sure that you have your own space and storage in the bathroom setting. A separate water closet is an important function of privacy and comfort, and separate sinks a very handy time saver.

BACKYARD BLISS A fixed picture window attests to the private setting beyond. When you own an extensive backyard, why not enjoy it from many vantage points? *Photography by Dave Adams Photography, Courtesy of Joyce Hoshall Interiors*

COMFORTS OF HOME A fireside retreat offers a place to unwind before or after a good long soak. *Courtesy of Kimberly Petruska Designs; Carol Koenig Interior Designer; Cindy Massa Design Elements*

Courtesy of Marrol's Hotel, Bratislava, Slovakia

spa tip

Quick-Change Artist

The look of your bathroom can be quickly and drastically changed with new curtains, throw rugs, towels, and accessories like soaps and candles. Try a little statuary, and if sunlight allows, a few houseplants. Plants love the steamy warm atmosphere of the bath as much as you do.

TREAT YOUR TOES Carpeting adds warmth to a bath suite, making the act of leaving a full tub a little less regrettable on a cold winter day. *Courtesy of Reynolds Gualco Architecture-Interior Design*

FAR EAST An Asian sensibility is captured with shoji screen and the cabinetry finish. *Dave Adams Photography, Courtesy of Reynolds Gualco Architecture-Interior Design*

CORNER TIME-OUT Commanding a full half of the space afforded by a master-suite addition, this master-bath suite revolves around the luxuries of a corner whirlpool tub and a glass-enclosed shower. *Courtesy of Shasta Smith*

spa tip

Bath Teas

There's more to tea than drinking when it comes to the bath. Herbal baths, particularly with teas, have been long in use not only for their relaxing and restorative properties, but for tackling everything from skin conditions to the fight of the common cold. In some cases, aromatherapy oils are combined to add that sense of romance, but regardless, taking a tea bath is a loving thing to do for your body.

For a tea bath, first choose the desired effect—relaxation, muscle/joint relief, skin condition treatment, etc.—and then purchase the appropriate tea blends from your herbal store. There are many mixtures and effects to choose from. Mix the teas in a cloth bag and boil in a large pot of water on the stove for about thirty minutes (like a giant tea bag!). Draw your bath to the hottest temperature you feel comfortable soaking, and then mix in the tea concoction. The water will take on the color of the tea. Now you're ready to soak away your troubles.

NOTE: Some people have sensitivities to varied herbal products; this should be explored before taking a tea bath.

STEPPING STONES Rock tile helps create the sense that one is following a stream back to an organic shower and pond-sized hot-tub. Natural light from sliding glass doors enhances the atmosphere of a healthful nature retreat. *Courtesy of Shasta Smith*

Candles, Colors, and Moods

Many a bather has taken advantage of candlelight to enhance the soaking experience. But can candles provide more than just a marvelous ambient glow? Some believe that candles are related to the world of the mind, body, and spirit, and that the color of the candle you choose is said to do much for your desire for rejuvenation. So next time, match your wick with your wishes!

PURITY invites the spiritual world, wisdom, and truth

PROTECTION fends off negativity and danger

LOVE, PASSION invites desire, excitement, and warm energy

LOVE, FRIENDSHIP invites affection

TRANQUILITY invites good health, peace of mind, and restores patience

PROSPERITY good luck and fertility will follow

POWER an elegant color of kings and queens, for use with meditation

FOCUS makes things clear, helps concentration, much success

ENCOURAGEMENT, ATTRACTION stimulates those around you and promotes positive interation

Cleanse Me!

On a particularly hot day, temperature or emotional, float slices of lemon in a hot bath or suspend them with a bar of mild soap while the water is running in a hot shower. As the water runs, close your eyes, concentrate on cleansing, and say:

Wash away my insecurities
Cleanse me from all doubt.
Wash away my worries,
Cleanse me! I cry out.

CORNER OFFICE A corner tub plays a central role in a room-sized master bath. *Courtesy of Toll Brothers, Inc.*

EVERYDAY ITALIAN A fully customized master suite has his-and-hers vanities capped in Rosa Verona marble, a large, frameless glass shower, and a whirlpool tub in the center next to a bay window. *Photography by Morris Gindi, Courtesy of Realm Designs, Inc.*

Keep yourself clean and bright. You are the window through which you must see the world.

GEORGE BERNARD SHAW
CRITIC/PLAYWRIGHT

Resource Guide

Designers

All American Design & Furnishings, Inc.
Folsom, California
916-987-7370
www.AllAmericanDesignandFurnishings.com

Atlanta Design & Build
Marietta, Georgia
770-565-8999
www.atlantadesignbuild.com

Benning Design Associates, Inc.
Sacramento, California
916-448-8120
www.benningdesign.com

a karen black company
Oklahoma City, Oklahoma
405-858-8333
www.akarenblackcompany.com

Design Elements, LPD
Allentown, Pennsylvania
610-437-3303
www.designelementshome.com

DiLeonardo International, Inc.
Warwick, Rhode Island
401-732-2900
www.dileonardo.com

Divine Kitchens, LLC
Westborough, Massachusetts
508-366-5670
www.divinekitchens.com

Directions in Design, Inc.
Long Valley, New Jersey
908-852-4228
www.directionsindesigninc.com

Maureen Fiori, Allied Member, ASID
Franklin Lakes, New Jersey
201-848-8188

Hermitage Kitchen Design Gallery
Nashville, Tennessee
615-843-3310
www.hermitagelighting.com

Joyce Hoshall Interiors
Folsom, California
916-765-7538
www.hoshallsfolsom.com

Interior Designs by Ria, LLC
Long Branch, New Jersey
732-571-1171
www.designs by ria.com

Stephen Francis Jones
Marina Del Ray, California
310-822-3822
www.sfjones.com

Kimberly Petruska Designs
Emmaus, Pennsylvania
610-966-5836
www.KimberlyPetruska.com

Lee Kimball
Winchester, Massachusetts
781-838-6100
www.leekimball.com

Carol Koenig Interior Designer
Allentown, Pennsylvania
610-439-3882

National Kitchen and Bath Association
Hackettstown, New Jersey
908-813-3792
www.nkba.org

Plumberry Designs, Inc.
Florham Park, New Jersey
973-966-1162
www.plumberry.net

Realm Designs, Inc.
Warren, New Jersey
908-753-3939
www.realmdesignsinc.com

Reynolds Gualco Architecture-Interior
Design
Sacramento, California
916-456-3720
www.rgaid.com

Shasta Smith
Sacramento, California
916-871-2892
www.ShastaSmith.com

SF Jones Architects, Inc.
Marina Del Rey, California
310-882-3822
www.sfjones.com

Manufacturers & Retailers

Aquapal U.S.A.
San Mateo, California
650-576-2783
www.aquapalusa.com

Aquatic Industries, Inc.
Leander, Texas
800-555-5324
www.aquaticwhirlpools.com

Diamond Spas
760 S. 104th St.
Bloomfield, Colorado
800-951-7727

DuraSupreme Cabinetry
Howard Lake, Minnesota
320-543-3872

Eldorado Stone
www.eldoradostone.com

Jacuzzi Whirlpool Bath
Chino, California
800-288-4002
www.jacuzzi.com

Julien, Troy Adams Design™
West Hollywood, California
310-657-1400
www.julien.ca

Kohler
Kohler, Wisconsin
800-456-4537
www.kohler.com

Lacava, LLC
Chicago, Illinois
312-666-4873
www.lacava.com

LimeStone Gallery
London, England, SW8 1SS
44 (0) 20 7735 8555
www.limestonegallery.com

Moen, Inc.
North Olmstead, Ohio
440-962-2000
www.moen.com

MTI Whirlpools, Inc.
Sugar Hill, Georgia
800-783-8827
www.mtiwhirlpools.com

Porcher©American Standard
Chandler, Arizona
800-359-3261
www.porcher-us.com

ThermaSol
West Coast, 800-776-0711
East Coast, 800-631-1601
www.thermasol.com

Wellborn Forest
Alexander City, Alabama
800-846-2562
www.wellbornforest.com

Builders

Barna Log Homes
Oneida, Tennessee
1-800-962-4734
www.barnahomes.com

Gastineau Log Homes, Inc.
New Bloomfield, Missouri
800-654-9253
www.oakloghome.com

Golden Eagle Log Homes, Inc.
Wisconsin Rapids, Wisconsin
800-270-5025
www.goldeneagleloghomes.com

Hearthstone, Inc.
Dandridge, Tennessee
800-247-4442
www.hearthstonehomes.com

Toll Brothers, Inc.
Horsham, Pennsylvania
215-938-8000
www.tollbrothers.com

Hospitality Suites

The Log House & Homestead
Vergas, Minnesota
800-342-2318
www.loghousebb.com

The Inn at Stockbridge
Stockbridge, Massachusetts
888-466-7865
www.stockbridgeinn.com

The following hotel properties are featured in this book. They would be delighted to host you in one of their beautiful master-bath suites.

Aegean Suites Hotel
Megali Ammos, Kiathos Island, Greece

Aka Hotel Resort & Spa
Hua Hin, Thailand

Albergo Piet
Pietransanta, Italy

Anatara Resort & Spa Golden Triangle
Chiang Rai, Thailand

Aquapura Douro Valley
Lemego, Portugal

Ashdown Park Hotel
East Sussex, England

Auberge Carmel
Monterey, California

The Bale Resort & Spa
Denpasur, Bali, Indonesia

The Bath Priory Hotel
Berkshire, England

Belle Epoque
Baden Baden, Germany

Blanket Bay
Queenstown, New Zealand

Ca Sagredo Hotel
Venice, Italy

Casa Que Canta
Zihuatanejo, Mexico

Chateau Beauvallon
Mont Tremblant, Quebec, Canada

Chateau de Fere
Fere En Tardenois, France

Coco Palm Resort Dhuni Kolhu
Mali, Maldives

Cortijo Soto Real
Seville, Spain

Costwold House Hotel
Chipping Campden, England

Die Hirschgrasse Heidelberg
Heidelberg, Germany

Discovery at Marigot Bay
St. Lucia

Dream of Africa
Malindi, Kenya, Africa

Eichardts Private Hotel
Queenstown, New Zealand

Elba Palace Hotel
Fuerteventura Island, Spain

Evanson 6 Senses
Sultanate of Oman, Oman, Middle East

Filadelfia Coffee Plantation
Antigua, Guatemala

The Forbury Hotel
Berkshire, England

The Fortress-Galle
Galle, Sri Lanka

The G
Galway, Ireland

Gaia Hotel
Quepos, Costa Rica

Goodstone Estate
Middleburg, Virginia

Grand Hotel Majestic
Milan, Italy

Grasmere Lodge
Christchurch, New Zealand

Hacienda Santos Alamos
Sonora, Mexico

Harbour Village
Beach Club Netherland Antilles, Bonaire

Hotel De La Paix
Siem Reap, Cambodia

Hotel Mas Passamaner
Le Selva Del Camp, Tarragona Prov. Spain

Hotel San Georgio
PortoFino, Italy

Hoteldorf Gruner Baum
Bad Gastein, Austria

Hotelito Desconodico
Puerto Vallarta, Mexico

Huka Lodge
Taupo, New Zealand

I Casali di Monticchio
Allerno, Italy

Inkaterra
Manchu Picchu, Peru

Inn of 5 Graces
Santa Fe, New Mexico

Inn of Great Neck
Great Neck, New York

Island Hideaway Resort & Spa
Dhonakulhi, Maldives

Katitche Point Guesthouse
The Valley, British Virgin Islands

Kristinia Lech
Lech, Austria

Krone Assmannshausen
Rudensheim, Germany

Labiz Silhouette
Make, Kenya, Africa

Langshott Manor
London, England

La Pleta Hotel & Spa
Barcelona, Spain

Larson Place Hotel
Hong Kong, China

La Sultana 'Marrakech' Hotel & Spa
Marrakech, Africa

lebua State Tower
State Tower, Thailand

Le Hostellerie Marechal
Colmar, France

Le Hotel Regina
Warsaw, Poland

Loch Torridon Country House Hotel
Achnasheen, England

Losari Coffee Plantation
Magelang, Indonesia

The Luxe Manor
Hong Kong, China

Manor on Golden Pond
Manchester, New Hampshire

Marrol's Hotel
Bratislava, Slovakia

Montana Art Deco Hotel
Lucerne, Switzerland

Mykonos Grand Hotel & Resort
Mykonos, Greece

Nafplia Palace Hotel & Resort
Greece

Ngala Game Reserve
Skukuza, South Africa

The Oberoi Amarvilas
Uttar Pradesh, India

Oberoi Bali
Bali, Indonesia

The Oberoi Mauritius
Mauritius, Indian Ocean

Oberoi Rajvilas
Jaipur, India

Oberoi Vanyavilas
Sawai Madhopur, Rajasthan,India

Old Bahama Bay
West End, Bahamas

Parisi
San Diego, California

Petit Palais Hotel de Charm
Milan, Italy

Pimalai Resort & Spa
Krabi, Thailand

Posada de la Casa del Abad
Palencia, Castilla Y Leon Province, Spain

Post Ranch
Monterey, California

Qualia
Hayman Island, Australia

The Raj Palace
Jaipur, India

Relais Dell'Orologio
Pisa, Italy

Residenza Del Moro
Firenze, Italy

Riverside
Prague, Poland

The Sandpiper
Bridgetown, Barbados, Caribbean

Savoy Moscow Hotel
Moscow, Russia

Sila Evanson Hideaway & Spa at Samui
Koh Samui Suratthani, Thailand

Sivoy Punta Cana Beach
Punta Cana, Dominican Republic

Solitaire Lodge
Rotorua, New Zealand

Stoke Park Club
London, England

Telegraff
Tallinn, Estonia

Tylney Hall
Southampton, England

Villa Crespi
Orta San Giulio, Italy

Villa Le Scale
Anacapri, Italy

Villa Rolundi Gourmet Beach
Cancun, Mexico

Photographers

Scott Amundson Photography
Eagan, Minnesota
651-454-3051
www.amundsonphoto.com

Dave Adams Photography
Winters, California
916-601-0852
www.daveadamsphotography.com

Tom Beckering Photography
Truckee, California
email: tomntahoe@prodigy.net

Dave Henry Photography
Roseville, California
916-321-1411

Christopher Ray Photography
Del Mar, California
www.Chrisrayphoto.com

Roger Wade Photography
Swan Lake, Montana
406-886-2793
www.rogerwadestudio.com

Peter Wnek
Meridian, Connecticut
www.peterwnekphoto.com

William Wright Photography
Seattle, Washington
www.williamwrightphoto.com

Joe Zugcic
Morganville, New Jersey
732-536-3288